EMBARRASSED

by Charly Haley

The Child's World®
childsworld.com

Published by The Child's World®
1980 Lookout Drive • Mankato, MN 56003-1705
800-599-READ • www.childsworld.com

Photographs ©: Shutterstock Images, cover,
1, 9, 10, 22 (bottom left); Nicolas McComber/
iStockphoto, 5, 6; Monkey Business Images/
Shutterstock Images, 13; iStockphoto, 14, 17, 21,
22 (top right); Valeriya Popova/Shutterstock
Images, 18; Donna Ellen Coleman/Shutterstock
Images, 22 (top left); Dipak Shelare/
Shutterstock Images, 22 (bottom right)

Design Elements: Shutterstock Images

ISBN Hardcover: 9781503828087
ISBN Paperback: 9781622434688
LCCN: 2018944230

Printed in the United States of America
PA02395

ABOUT THE AUTHOR

Charly Haley is a writer and
children's book editor who lives in
Minnesota. Aside from reading and
writing, she enjoys music, yoga,
and spending time with friends
and family.

CONTENTS

JACK IS EMBARRASSED

Jack's teacher wrote a math problem on the board. She asked Jack to complete the problem. Jack was not sure he could solve it.

Jack got the wrong answer. Jack felt embarrassed. He looked down. He wanted to hide. But his teacher told him that it was okay. Jack felt better.

FEELING EMBARRASSED

People feel embarrassed when they **worry** about what other people think about them.

Some people might worry after they get a new haircut. Or they might think people will laugh after they spill on their shirt. Those thoughts can make people feel embarrassed.

You might feel embarrassed if people are mean to you. You could feel embarrassed if you make a **mistake**.

THINK ABOUT IT

Can you think of a time when you felt embarrassed?

13

Embarrassed people might **blush**.
They could look down. They might
want to hide.

DEALING WITH EMBARRASSMENT

Everyone feels embarrassed sometimes. When you feel embarrassed you can talk to a parent, teacher, or friend. They can help you feel better.

You might want to be alone when you feel embarrassed. Try to **calm** yourself down. Embarrassing things often seem worse than they really are.

Try your best to not make other people feel embarrassed. Don't laugh if you see someone who seems embarrassed. Be nice to other people.

WHO IS EMBARRASSED?

Can you tell who is embarrassed? Turn to page 24 for the answer.

A

B

C

D

GLOSSARY

blush (BLUSH) A blush is when someone's face turns red because they are embarrassed. When Sasha's classmates teased her, it made her blush.

calm (KALM) To feel calm is to feel peaceful. Ben is calm when he reads a book.

mistake (miss-TAKE) Someone makes a mistake if they do something wrong. Everyone makes a mistake sometimes.

worry (WORR-ee) People worry when something bad happens or when they think something bad will happen. Bad weather can make people worry.

TO LEARN MORE

Books

Dalton, Alexandra. *When I'm Embarrassed*. Vestal, NY: Village Earth Press, 2014.

Dinmont, Kerry. *Dan's First Day of School: A Book about Emotions*. Mankato, MN: The Child's World, 2018.

Millar, Goldie. *F Is for Feelings*. Minneapolis, MN: Free Spirit Publishing, 2014.

Web Sites

Visit our Web site for links about being embarrassed: **childsworld.com/links**

Note to Parents, Teachers, and Librarians: We routinely verify our Web links to make sure they are safe and active sites. So encourage your readers to check them out!

INDEX